DATE DUE

GAYLORD			PRINTED IN U.S.A.

SQUISHY, MISTY, DAMP & MUDDY

The In-Between World of Wetlands

Molly Cone

Sierra Club Books for Children • San Francisco

The Sierra Club, founded in 1892 by John Muir, has devoted itself to the study and protection of the earth's scenic and ecological resources — mountains, wetlands, woodlands, wild shores and rivers, deserts and plains. The publishing program of the Sierra Club offers books to the public as a nonprofit educational service in the hope that they may enlarge the public's understanding of the Club's basic concerns. The Sierra Club has some sixty chapters in the United States and in Canada. For information about how you may participate in its programs to preserve wilderness and the quality of life, please address inquiries to Sierra Club, 730 Polk Street, San Francisco, CA 94109.

B&T   15.95 — 10-20-97

E574.32
CON
c.1

Acknowledgments For their helpful critiques of early manuscript drafts, the author wishes to thank the following: Brian Lynn, Washington Department of Ecology, Olympia, WA; Neil Maine, Special Projects Coordinator for the Coastal Studies and Technology Center, Seaside High School, Seaside, OR; Lynn Pruzan, educator, Seattle, WA; Mary Roberts, environmentalist, Auburn, WA; Erik C. Stockdale, Wetlands Specialist, Washington Department of Ecology, Northwest Regional Office, Bellevue, WA; Sidnee Wheelwright, Adopt-A-Stream Foundation, Everett, WA; and Bob Zeigler, Wetlands Biologist, Habitat Program, Washington Department of Fish and Wildlife, Olympia, WA.

Library of Congress Cataloging-in-Publication Data

Cone, Molly.
    Squishy, misty, damp & muddy: the in-between world of wetlands / Molly Cone.
        p.   cm.
    Summary: Describes the damp environment of wetlands, the useful purposes they serve, and the plants and animals that inhabit them.
    ISBN 0-87156-480-7 (alk. paper)
    1. Wetland fauna — Juvenile literature. 2. Wetland plants — Juvenile literature. 3. Wetlands — Juvenile literature. 4. Wetland ecology — Juvenile literature. [1. Wetlands. 2. Wetland ecology. 3. Ecology.] I. Title.
QH87.3.C65 1996
574.5'26325 — dc20   95-39891

Book and jacket design: Bonnie Smetts
Printed in Singapore
10 9 8 7 6 5 4 3 2 1

For Nathan, who likes books that tell you something,
and for Hannah, who just likes books

If it looks like a river flowing with grass . . .

or a forest of trees standing knee-deep in water . . .

or a mossy green field that trembles when the wind blows . . .

it probably isn't

a river or a forest or a field.

Most likely, it's a wetland —

a place that's neither all land

nor all water.

It's a world in between.

Marshes, swamps, bogs, sloughs,

lagoons, potholes, mudflats —

all these are wetlands.

A roadside ditch filled with

wagging cattails is a wetland.

So is a muddy pond

alive with croaking frogs.

There are freshwater wetlands
and saltwater wetlands,
coastal wetlands and inland wetlands.
There are wetlands scattered
over the entire earth.

Some wetlands stretch
several football fields long.
Others aren't much bigger
than a good-size mud puddle.
Some wetlands stay wet all the time;
others are wet only part of the time.

Wetland soil is different
from other soils.
It's full of water, low in oxygen,
squishy to walk on,
and sometimes rather smelly.

What grows in this watery ground
is different, too.
Five thousand kinds of trees
and other plants
thrive in wetland soil.
But not all these plants
are found in every wetland.
What grows in each depends
on the kind of wetland it is.

Marshes have no trees,
but they're filled with many other plants,
including grasses, sedges,
cattails, and water lilies.

Water-loving trees such as cypress,

tamarack, and mangrove

grow in swamps.

Orchids love swamps, too.

(And so do alligators!)

Bogs are covered mostly

with spongy mosses.

They're also places where

wild cranberries grow

and sticky sundew plants

capture insects.

These and other types of wetlands

are home to many different creatures.

Bird-watchers visit wetlands
to see the many hundreds
of different kinds of birds
that regularly fly in
to rest, nest, and feed.
More than half
of all the bird species
that live in the United States
depend on wetlands.

As many as 200 kinds of fish
live for all or part of their lives
in wetland ponds and streams.
And shrimp, oysters, clams,
and other shellfish
begin life in coastal wetlands.

15

16

Wetlands are favorite roaming places
for deer, elk, bears, and other mammals.
Beavers and muskrats are two mammals
that live their whole lives in wetlands.
Amphibians such as toads and newts,
which both swim and crawl,
also make their homes in wetlands.
Many kinds of turtles
and other reptiles do, too.

Wetland ponds are nurseries
for beetles, dragonflies,
and hundreds of other kinds of insects
that are food for other animal life.

In fact, more than half of all animals
breed, feed, raise their young,
or escape from hot or cold weather
in wetlands.

Everything, living or dead,

has value in a wetland.

In this watery world,

all things that come to an end

are part of a new beginning.

A handful of mud

scooped up from the bottom

of a wetland pond

is full of wetland history.

In it are the remains of fish, birds,

mammals, insects, grasses, leaves,

seeds, petals, and more.

These decaying bits

become part of the soil

that will nurture new generations.

Two hundred years ago,

wetlands covered more than

200 million acres of the United States.

That's bigger than

the whole state of Texas!

Most people looked upon

all those wet, muddy places

as "wastelands."

They saw no use for them

and no reason for saving them.

Many wetlands were drained and filled in.

They became fields of corn

or carrots or cabbages,

or were covered by

houses and barns.

They were hidden under roads

or piled high with garbage.

As towns and cities grew,
freeways, airports, and parking lots
were built on top of wetlands.
Shopping malls began to spring up
where water lilies used to grow
and tadpoles once played.

Most people hardly noticed
that the wetlands were disappearing.
They did begin to notice
other things, though —
things that worried them.
There were fewer birds in the trees
and fewer fish in the streams.
More roads were flooding when it rained.
More riverbanks were washing away.
More streams were drying up.

For a long time, almost no one

connected these problems

to the lost wetlands.

Then a few people,

and gradually a few more,

began to see what no one

had paid any attention to before —

the many things that wetlands do

to help the natural world stay in balance.

One of the important things wetlands do

is shelter and protect wildlife.

When a wetland is destroyed,

the many creatures that depend on it

for survival often disappear, too.

Wetlands also produce great quantities of

food for many animals, including humans.

Wetlands help protect populated areas
from both floods and droughts.

During rainy weather,
a wetland acts like an enormous sponge.
It catches and holds the excess water
that would otherwise
overflow roads and fields
and seep into houses.

During dry times,
a wetland's spongy soil
gradually releases its soaked-up water.
This water flows into brooks and streams,
keeping them from drying up
and keeping the fish in them from dying.

Wetland plants protect riverbanks
and help prevent shoreline erosion
by holding on to the earth
with their roots
and keeping the soil
from washing away.

Perhaps most remarkable of all,
wetlands can make dirty water
pure, fresh, and sparkling again.
The roots and stems
of wetland plants
act like filters,
catching dirt and pollutants
as rain or runoff water
flows over them.
The cleaned water
gradually seeps downward
until it reaches a layer of pools
deep underground.
These pools supply
our wells and reservoirs
with pure drinking water.

Today, more and more people
are discovering that wetlands
are wild and wonderful places
where you can not only find
ducks and deer,
beavers and butterflies,
toads and tadpoles —
you can have fun fishing, boating,
taking pictures, and just exploring.

With less than half
of our country's original wetlands left,
no one is calling them
"wastelands" anymore.
Saving and protecting these
squishy, misty, damp, and muddy places
is now everybody's job.
Because wetlands are
not just for cattails and water lilies,
not just for frogs and dragonflies,
not just for nature lovers
and bird-watchers.
Wetlands are for everyone.